THE LITTLE BLACK BOOK OF
CLASSIC
COCKTAILS

First published in Great Britain in 2018 by Pyramid,
an imprint of Octopus Publishing Group Ltd
Carmelite House, 50 Victoria Embankment, London EC4Y 0DZ
www.octopusbooks.co.uk

Distributed in the US by
Hachette Book Group
1290 Avenue of the Americas
4th and 5th Floors
New York, NY 10104

Distributed in Canada by
Canadian Manda Group
664 Annette St.
Toronto, Ontario, Canada M6S 2C8

ISBN 978-0-7537-3332-5

A CIP catalogue record for this book is available from the British Library

Printed and bound in China

10

Publisher: Lucy Pessell
Designer: Lisa Layton
Editor: Sarah Vaughan
Production Manager: Caroline Alberti

The measure that has been used in the recipes is based on a bar jigger, which is 25 ml (1 fl oz).
If preferred, a different volume can be used, providing the proportions are kept constant within a drink
and suitable adjustments are made to spoon measurements, where they occur.

Standard level spoon measurements are used in all recipes.
1 tablespoon = one 15 ml spoon
1 teaspoon = one 5 ml spoon

This book contains cocktails made with raw or lightly cooked eggs. It is prudent for more vulnerable people
to avoid uncooked or lightly cooked cocktails made with eggs.

Some of this material previously appeared in *501 Must-Drink Cocktails* and *Hamlyn All Colour Cookery
200 Classic Cocktails*.

THE LITTLE BLACK BOOK OF
CLASSIC
COCKTAILS

INTRODUCTION

Whether served at a glamorous cocktail party or as a precursor to a night out, cocktails lend an air of sophistication, glamour and – ultimately – fun.

There are hundreds and hundreds of different cocktails, some of which experience fleeting popularity before disappearing into obscurity, while others remain popular for decades, finding their way into the collection of must-know and definitely must-try "classics".

From the simple yet suave Old Fashioned, to the summer-time sharer Pimms Cocktail, *The Little Black Book of Classic Cocktails* contains a host of timeless and contemporary favourites, gathered together in a purse-sized collection.

CONTENTS

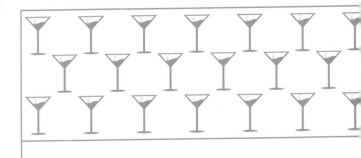

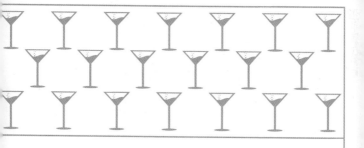

FIZZES,
HIGHBALLS &
COLLINSES

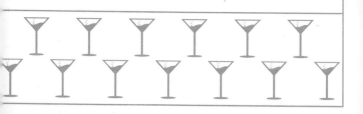

GIN CUCUMBER COOLER

2 measures gin
5 mint leaves
5 slices cucumber
3 measures apple juice
3 measures soda water
mint, to garnish

Add the gin, mint and cucumber to a glass and gently muddle.

Leave to stand for a couple of minutes, then add the apple juice, soda water and some ice cubes.

Garnish with a sprig of mint.

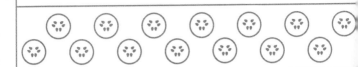

SEA BREEZE

2 measures vodka

4 measures cranberry juice

2 measures grapefruit juice

lime wedges, to garnish

Fill 2 highball glasses with ice cubes, pour over the vodka, cranberry juice and grapefruit juice and stir well.

Garnish with lime wedges.

TOM COLLINS

2 measures gin
1 measure sugar syrup
1 measure lemon juice
4 measures soda water

to garnish:
lemon wedge
black cherry

Put the gin, sugar syrup and lemon juice into a cocktail shaker and fill with ice cubes.

Shake then strain into a glass full of ice cubes and top up with the soda water.

Garnish with a lemon wedge and a cherry.

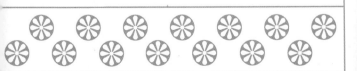

CAMOMILE COLLINS

2 measures gin
1 camomile tea bag
1 measure lemon juice
1 measure sugar syrup
4 measures soda water
lemon slice, to garnish

Pour the gin into a glass and add the tea bag. Stir the tea bag and gin together until the gin is infused with camomile flavour, about 5 minutes.

Remove the tea bag and fill the glass with ice cubes

Add the remaining ingredients and garnish with a lemon slice.

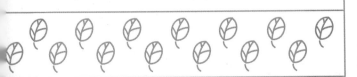

SINGAPORE SLING

2 measures gin
1 measure cherry brandy
½ measure Cointreau
½ measure Bénédictine
1 measure grenadine
1 measure lime juice
10 measures pineapple juice
1–2 dashes Angostura bitters

to garnish:
pineapple wedges
maraschino cherries

Half-fill a cocktail shaker with ice cubes and put some ice cubes into each highball glass. Add the remaining ingredients to the shaker and shake until a frost forms on the outside of the shaker.

Strain over the ice cubes into the glasses.

Garnish each one with a pineapple wedge and a maraschino cherry.

SEX ON THE BEACH

makes 2

2 measures vodka

2 measures peach schnapps

2 measures cranberry juice

2 measures orange juice

2 measures pineapple juice (optional)

to garnish:
lemon wedges
lime wedges

Put 8–10 ice cubes into a cocktail shaker and add the vodka, schnapps, cranberry juice, orange juice and pineapple juice (if used). Shake well.

Put 3–4 ice cubes into each highball glass, strain over the cocktail.

Garnish with lemon and lime wedges.

FINO HIGHBALL

1 measure gin
1 measure fino sherry
2 teaspoons passion
fruit syrup
4 slices clementine
2 slices lemon
2 measures low-calorie
tonic water
lemon wedge, to
garnish

Muddle the fruit in a cocktail shaker, add the gin, sherry and passion fruit syrup.

Fill cocktail shaker with ice cubes and shake, then strain, into a glass.

Add the tonic water, fill the glass with crushed ice and garnish with a lemon wedge.

LONG ISLAND ICED TEA

1 measure vodka
1 measure gin
1 measure white rum
1 measure tequila
1 measure Cointreau
1 measure lemon juice
cola, to top up
lemon slices, to garnish

Put the vodka, gin, rum, tequila, Cointreau and lemon juice in a cocktail shaker with some ice cubes and shake to mix.

Strain into 2 highball glasses filled with ice cubes and top up with cola.

Garnish with lemon slices.

GINNY GIN FIZZ

1 camomile tea bag
2 measures gin
1 measure sugar syrup
1 measure lemon juice
3 teaspoons egg white
3 measures soda water
lemon twist, to garnish

Place the tea bag and gin in a cocktail shaker and leave to infuse for 2 minutes. Remove the tea bag, add the sugar syrup, lemon juice and egg white.

Fill the shaker with ice cubes and shake and strain into a wine glass filled with ice cubes and top up with the soda water.

Garnish with a lemon twist.

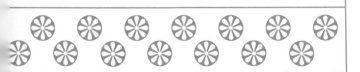

PIMMS COCKTAIL

makes 2

2 measures Pimm's
No. 1 Cup

2 measures gin

4 measures lemonade

4 measures ginger ale

to garnish:
cucumber strips
blueberries
orange slices

Fill 2 highball glasses with ice cubes. Add the all the ingredients, one by one in order, over the ice.

Garnish with cucumber strips, blueberries and orange slices.

MOJITO

makes 2

16 mint leaves, plus
sprigs to garnish

1 lime, cut into wedges

4 teaspoons cane sugar

5 measures white rum

soda water, to top up

Muddle the mint leaves, lime and sugar in the bottom of 2 highball glasses and fill with crushed ice.

Add the rum, stir and top up with soda water.

Garnish with mint sprigs and serve.

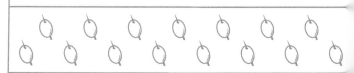

ORANGE BLOSSOM

makes 2

4 teaspoons almond syrup

8 orange slices, plus wedges to garnish

6 dashes Angostura bitters

4 measures pink grapefruit juice

Muddle half the orange slices and almond syrup in each glass. Fill the glasses with crushed ice and pour in the gin.

Stir, top up with the grapefruit juice and bitters and garnish with orange wedges.

Serve with straws.

BLOODY MARY

2 measures vodka
juice of ½ lemon
½ teaspoon horseradish sauce
2 drops Worcestershire sauce
1 drop Tabasco sauce
2 measures thick tomato juice
pinch of salt
pinch of cayenne pepper

to garnish:
celery stick, with leaves
lemon slice
green olives

Add some ice cubes into a cocktail shaker and pour over the vodka, lemon juice, horseradish, Worcestershire and Tabasco sauces, tomato juice. Shake until a frost forms.

Pour into a highball and add the salt and cayenne pepper.

Garnish with a celery stick, lemon slice and 3 olives.

PLANTER'S PUNCH

makes 2

4 measures Myer's Jamaican Planter's Punch rum

8 drops Angostura bitters

1 measure lime juice

4 measures chilled water

2 measures sugar syrup

to garnish:
orange slices
lime slices

Put the rum, bitters, lime juice, water and sugar syrup in a cocktail shaker and add some ice cubes.

Shake and strain into 2 chilled glasses and garnish with orange and lime slices.

SCREWDRIVER

1½ measures vodka
orange juice, to top up
¼ slices of orange, to
garnish

Add a few ice cubes into a
tumbler and pour the vodka
over them.

Top up with orange juice and
stir lightly.

Garnish with orange slice
quarters and serve with a
straw.

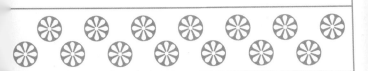

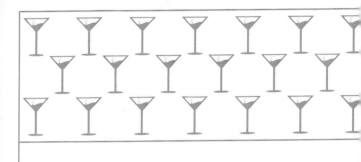

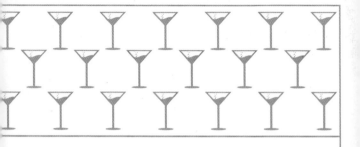

SPIRIT
FORWARDS

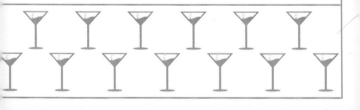

CLASSIC MARTINI

makes 2

1 measure dry vermouth
6 measures gin
stuffed green olives, to garnish

Put 10–12 ice cubes into a mixing glass.

Pour over the vermouth and gin and stir (never shake) vigorously and evenly without splashing.

Strain into 2 chilled Martini glasses and garnish each with a green olive.

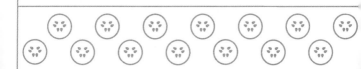

ABC
COCKTAIL

1 measure VSOP
Cognac

1 measure tawny port

2 teaspoons
maraschino liqueur

6 mint leaves, plus
extra, to garnish

Add all the ingredients to a
cocktail shaker.

Shake and strain into a glass
and garnish with a mint leaf.

LYCHEE MARTINI

2 measures vodka

3 lychees, plus extra, to garnish

1 measure Triple Sec

3 teaspoons lemon juice

Add all the ingredients to a cocktail shaker and muddle.

Shake, then strain into a Martini glass and garnish with a lychee.

MARTINEZ

2 measures gin

3 teaspoons sweet
vermouth

2 teaspoons orange
liqueur

2 dashes Angostura
bitters

orange twist, to garnish

Fill a glass with ice and add
the remaining ingredients.

Stir and garnish with an
orange twist.

GODMOTHER

3 measures vodka

1 measure Amaretto di Saronno

Put 4–6 cracked ice cubes into 2 old-fashioned glasses.

Add the vodka and Amaretto, and stir lightly to mix.

MANHATTAN

3 measures rye or bourbon whiskey

1 measure sweet vermouth

cocktail cherry, to garnish (optional)

Put 4–5 ice cubes into a mixing glass and pour the vermouth and whiskey over it.

Stir vigorously, then strain into a chilled cocktail glass.

Drop in a cocktail cherry, if you like.

NEGRONI

1 measure gin
1 measure sweet vermouth
1 measure Campari
orange wedge, to garnish

Fill a glass with ice cubes and add all the ingredients to a glass and stir.

Garnish with an orange wedge and serve.

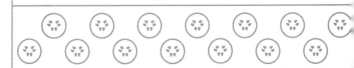

ZOMBIE

1 measure dark rum
1 measure white rum
½ measure golden rum
2 teaspoons over-proof rum
½ measure apricot brandy
1 teaspoon grenadine
juice of ½ lime
2 measures pineapple juice
½ measure sugar syrup

to garnish:
pineapple wedge and leaf
sugar

Put some ice cubes into a cocktail shaker with the dark, white and golden rums, apricot brandy, lime juice, grenadine, pineapple juice and sugar syrup and shake well.

Pour without straining into a chilled glass and float the over-proof rum on top.

Garnish with a pineapple wedge and leaf, and sprinkle a pinch of sugar over the top.

VESPER

3 measures gin

1 measure vodka

½ measure Lillet apéritif wine

lemon rind twist, to garnish

Put some ice cubes into a cocktail shaker with the gin, vodka and Lillet and shake well.

Strain into a chilled cocktail glass and add a lemon rind twist, to garnish.

VALENTINE MARTINI

makes 2

4 measures raspberry vodka

1 measure lime juice

2 dashes sugar syrup

12 raspberries, plus extra to garnish

lime rind spirals, to garnish

Half-fill a cocktail shaker with ice cubes. Add all the remaining ingredients and shake until a frost forms on the outside of the shaker.

Double-strain into 2 chilled Martini glasses and garnish with raspberries and lime rind spirals on cocktail sticks.

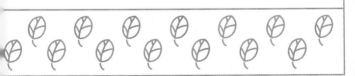

BRONX

1 measure gin

1 measure sweet vermouth

1 measure dry vermouth

2 measures orange juice

Put some cracked ice into a cocktail shaker and pour the gin, vermouths and orange juice over it. Shake to mix.

Strain into an old-fashioned glass over some ice cubes.

to garnish:

orange rind spiral

cocktail cherry (optional)

mint spring

Garnish with orange slices and a cocktail cherry, if you like.

VODKA GIBSON

1 measure vodka

½ measure dry vermouth

2 pearl onions, to garnish (optional)

Put some ice cubes into a cocktail shaker and add the vodka and vermouth.

Shake until a frost forms, then strain into a cocktail glass and garnish with 2 pearl onions on a cocktail stick, if you like.

GRASSHOPPER

2 measures crème de cacao

2 measures crème de menthe

mint sprigs, to garnish

Pour the crème de cacao into 2 Martini glasses.

Using the back of a bar spoon, float the crème de menthe over the crème de cacao to create a separate layer.

Garnish with mint sprigs.

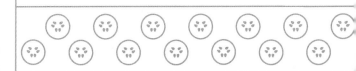

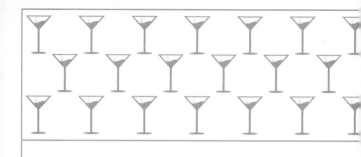

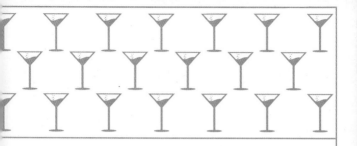

SOURS

DAIQUIRI

2 measures light rum
1 measure sugar syrup
1 measure lime juice
lime wedge, to garnish

Add all the ingredients to a cocktail shaker with some cubes of ice.

Shake and strain into a glass and garnish with a lime wedge.

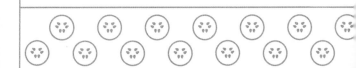

WHISKY SOUR

2 measures Scotch whisky

1 measure lemon juice

1 measure sugar syrup

to garnish:
lemon wedge
lemon rind spirals

Fill a cocktail shaker with ice cubes. Add the remaining ingredients and shake.

Strain into a glass filled with ice cubes, garnish with a lemon wedge and a lemon rind spiral.

MOSCOW MULE

2 measures vodka
juice of 2 limes
ginger beer, to top up

to garnish:
lime slice
mint sprig

Put some cracked ice into a highball glass.

Add the vodka and lime juice, stir and top up with ginger beer.

Garnish with a lime slice and a mint sprig.

SOUTHSIDE

2 measures gin
4 teaspoons lime juice
4 teaspoons sugar syrup
5 mint leaves, plus extra,
to garnish

Add some ice cubes with all the ingredients to a cocktail shaker.

Shake and strain into a glass and garnish with a mint leaf.

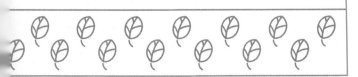

MOON RIVER

makes 2

1 measure dry gin

1 measure apricot brandy

1 measure Cointreau

½ measure Galliano

½ measure lemon juice

maraschino cherries, to garnish

Put some ice cubes into a cocktail shaker. Pour the gin, apricot brandy, Cointreau, Galliano and lemon juice over the ice.

Shake, then strain into 2 large chilled Martini glasses and garnish each with a maraschino cherry.

MARGARITA

to frost the glass:
1 lime wedge
rock salt

Frost the rim of a Margarita glass by moistening it with a lime wedge, then pressing it into the salt.

2 measures Herradura Reposado tequila
1 measure lime juice
1 measure Triple Sec
lime slice, to garnish

Put some ice cubes into a cocktail shaker with the tequila, lime juice and Triple Sec. Shake well.

Strain into the prepared glass and garnish with a lime slice.

COSMOPOLITAN

1½ measures lemon vodka

4 teaspoons Triple Sec

3 teaspoons lime juice

1 measure cranberry juice

lime wedge, to garnish

Add all the ingredients to a cocktail shaker.

Shake and strain into a glass and garnish with a lime wedge.

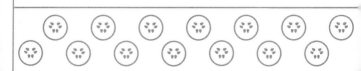

WHITE
LADY

1 measure gin

1 measure Cointreau

1 measure lemon juice

lemon rind twist, to
garnish (optional)

Pour the gin, Cointreau and
lemon juice into a cocktail
shaker and shake well.

Strain into a chilled Martini
glass and garnish with a
lemon rind twist, if you like.

MAI TAI

2 measures golden rum
½ measure orange Curaçao
½ measure orgeat syrup
juice of 1 lime
2 teaspoons Wood's Navy Rum

to garnish:
lime rind
mint sprig

Put some ice cubes into a cocktail shaker with the golden rum, Curaçao, orgeat syrup and lime juice and shake well.

Strain over crushed ice into an old-fashioned glass, float the Navy rum on top and garnish with lime rind and a mint sprig.

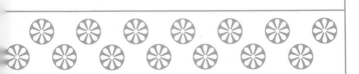

STRAWBERRY DAIQUIRI

2 measures golden rum
2 measures lime juice
3 strawberries, hulled
dash of strawberry syrup
6 mint leaves, plus a sprig to garnish
strawberry slice, to garnish

Muddle the strawberries, syrup and mint leaves in the bottom of a cocktail shaker.

Add the rum and lime juice, shake with ice and double-strain into a chilled Martini glass.

Garnish with a strawberry slice and a sprig of mint.

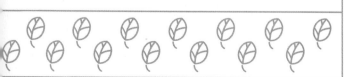

AVIATION

2 measures gin
½ measure maraschino liqueur
½ measure lemon juice
cocktail cherry, to garnish

Put some ice cubes into a cocktail shaker with the gin, maraschino liqueur and lemon juice.

Shake well and double strain into a chilled Martini glass.

Garnish with a cocktail cherry on a cocktail stick.

CORPSE REVIVER

2 measures brandy
1 measure Calvados
1 measure sweet vermouth
apple slice, to garnish

Put some cracked ice into a cocktail shaker and add the brandy, Calvados and vermouth and shake until a frost forms.

Strain into a glass and garnish with an apple slice

RED RUM

makes 2

1 measure sloe gin

4 measures Bacardi
8-year-old rum

1 measure lemon juice

1 measure vanilla syrup

handful of redcurrants,
plus extra to garnish

Muddle the redcurrants and sloe
gin together in a cocktail shaker.

Add the rum, lemon juice, vanilla
syrup and some ice cubes.

Shake and double-strain into
2 chilled Martini glasses and
garnish with redcurrants.

GIMLET

2 measures gin
1 measure lime cordial
juice of ¼ lime
½ measure water
lime rind spiral, to
garnish

Put the gin and lime cordial
into a mixing glass, fill up
with ice cubes and stir well.

Strain into a chilled cocktail
glass and add the water and
lime juice into the cocktail.

Garnish with a lime rind
spiral.

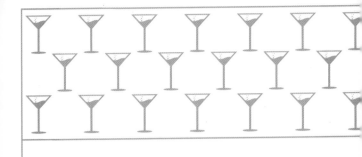

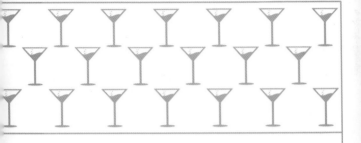

OLD
FASHIONEDS

OLD FASHIONED

2 measures bourbon
1 dash orange bitters
1 dash Angostura bitters
1 teaspoon sugar syrup
orange twist, to garnish

Half-fill a glass with ice cubes. Add all the ingredients to the glass and stir for 1 minute.

Fill the glass with more ice cubes and garnish with with an orange twist.

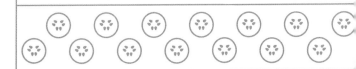

VODKA SAZERAC

2 measures vodka
3 drops Pernod
2 drops Angostura bitters
1 sugar cube
lemonade, to top up

Put the sugar cube into an old-fashioned glass and shake the bitters onto it.

Add the Pernod and swirl it around to coat the inside of the glass. Drop in the ice cubes and pour in the vodka.

Top up with lemonade and stir gently.

RITZ OLD FASHIONED

to frost the glass:
lime juice
caster sugar

Frost the rim of a cocktail glass by dipping it into the lime juice, then pressing it into the sugar.

1½ measures bourbon whiskey
½ measure Grand Marnier
1 dash lemon juice
1 dash Angostura bitters
orange or lemon rind spiral, to garnish

Put crushed ice into a cocktail shaker and add the bourbon, Grand Marnier, lemon juice and bitters.

Shake to mix, then strain into the prepared glass and garnish with an orange or lemon rind spiral.

75

RUM OLD FASHIONED

makes 2

4 measures white rum
1 measure dark rum
2 dashes Angostura bitters
2 dashes lime bitters
2 teaspoons caster sugar
1 measure water
orange rind twists, to garnish

Stir 1 ice cube with a dash of both bitters, 1 teaspoon sugar and half the water in each old-fashioned glass until the sugar has dissolved.

Add the white rum, stir and add the remaining ice cubes. Add the dark rum and stir again.

Garnish each glass with an orange rind twist.

OLD FASHIONED AT DUSK

2 teaspoons Islay whisky

2 measures tequila

1 teaspoon agave syrup

2 dashes Angostura bitters

orange twist, to garnish

Add all the ingredients to an old-fashioned glass full of ice cubes and stir.

Garnish with an orange twist.

RHETT BUTLER

2 measures bourbon whiskey
4 measures cranberry juice
2 tablespoons sugar syrup
1 tablespoon lime juice
lime slices, to garnish

Put some ice cubes into a cocktail shaker with the bourbon, cranberry juice, sugar syrup and lime juice and shake well.

Strain an old-fashioned glass filled with ice cubes.

Garnish with lime slices and serve with straws.

RUSTY NAIL

1½ measures Scotch whisky

1 measure Drambuie

Fill an old-fashioned glass with ice cubes and pour the whisky and Drambuie over them.

Stir gently before serving.

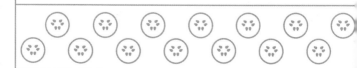

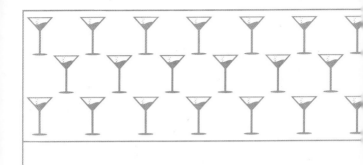

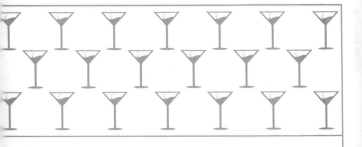

CHAMPAGNE
& PROSECCO

BELLINI

½ ripe white peach

2 teaspoons sugar syrup

5 measures Prosecco, chilled

Put the peach and sugar syrup into a food processor or blender and blend until smooth.

Strain into a flute glass and top with the Prosecco.

ROSSINI

4 strawberries
2 teaspoons sugar syrup
5 measures Prosecco, chilled

Put the strawberries and sugar syrup into a food processor or blender and blend until smooth.

Strain into a flute glass and top with the Prosecco.

FRENCH 75

1 measure gin

3 teaspoons lemon juice

3 teaspoons sugar syrup

4 measures
Champagne, chilled

lemon twist, to garnish

Add the gin, lemon juice and sugar syrup to a cocktail shaker and shake.

Strain into a flute glass and top up with the Champagne.

Garnish with a lemon twist.

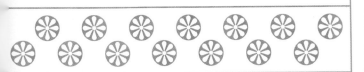

BUCKS FIZZ

2 measures fresh orange juice, chilled

1 measure sloe gin, chilled

2 measures Prosecco, chilled

orange twist, to garnish

Pour all the ingredients into a flute glass and garnish with an orange twist.

SBAGLIATO

1 measure Campari

1 measure sweet
vermouth

2 measures Prosecco,
chilled

orange slice, to garnish

Fill a glass with ice cubes
and add the Campari, sweet
vermouth and Prosecco and stir.

Garnish with an orange slice.

CLASSIC CHAMPAGNE COCKTAIL

1 measure brandy

1 sugar cube

1–2 dashes Angostura bitters

chilled Champagne, to top up

orange slice, to garnish

Saturate the sugar cube with the bitters, then drop it into a chilled cocktail glass or Champagne flute.

Add the brandy, top up with chilled Champagne and garnish with an orange slice.

COBBLER FIZZ

1 measure fino sherry

3 slices mandarin

2 raspberries, plus extra to garnish

2 teaspoons sugar syrup

4 measures Prosecco, chilled

Add the mandarin, raspberries and sugar syrup to a cocktail shaker and muddle.

Add the sherry and shake and strain into a flute glass before topping up with the Prosecco.

Garnish with a raspberry.

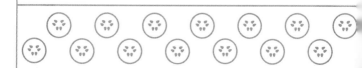

CHAMPAGNE JULEP

1 measure brandy

2 mint sprigs, plus extra to garnish

1 tablespoon sugar syrup

crushed ice

Champagne, to top up

Muddle the mint with the sugar syrup in a highball glass.

Fill the glass with crushed ice, then add the brandy.

Top up with Champagne, stir gently and garnish with extra mint sprigs.

GRAND MIMOSA

1 measure Grand
Marnier

2 measures orange
juice, chilled

Champagne, chilled, to
top up

Pour the Grand Marnier and
chilled orange juice into a
Champagne flute and top up
with chilled Champagne.

PICTURE ACKNOWLEDGEMENTS

cover and interior icons:
Noun Project byarif fajar yulianto;
Marco Livolsi; Royyan Wijaya;
Thomas Bruck.

interior images:
123RF alex_l 81; Brent Hofacker
68; Oleksandr Prokopenko 25.
Octopus Publishing Group
Jonathan Kennedy 9, 12, 17, 34, 39,
51, 54, 59, 62, 73, 85, 88, 93;
Stephen Conroy 20, 31, 42, 47, 67.
Unsplash Marc Babin 76.